# Imparting a
## Father's
### Blessing

GREG VIOLI

Published by: Der Überwinder-Verlag, Astrid-Lindgren-Str. 8,
32107 Bad Salzuflen, Germany.

Cover Design: 2016 by Jemima Gassmann- Buro fur Grafik Design
Book Design: 2016 by "THERISMOS" Sp. z o.o., ul. Sztabowa 32, 50-984
Wroclaw, Poland.

ISBN: 978-3-944038-20-9

Books are available to order (in multiple languages) from:
Der Ueberwinder Verlag
Astrid-Lindgren-Str. 8
32107 Bad Salzuflen
www.ueberwinder-verlag.de

For more information about the author and this message please visit this website:
www.greg-violi.com

From this website you can contact and schedule speaking engagements
with Pator Greg Violi. You can also find videos and sermons from
Pastor Greg Violi on  the same website.

# THE FATHER'S BLESSING

I am going to share with you what God the Father has been teaching me over the last 25 years. We have seen over 10,000 people changed as we give a Father's blessing, Father God comes and gives us his mighty presence and pure love as we minister blessing in His name. It is an amazing sight to behold. The radical transformed lives that occur as a direct result of giving a 5 or 10 minute prayer of blessing is absolutely miraculous.

In this brief booklet I will discuss how the Lord has taught me over the last 25 years how to impart the blessing of a father to anyone that will allow me to stand in for their earthly father, just doing what they should have done for their children in the form of blessing them. Within the Jewish culture, there is a special ceremony for a boy and a girl, in this ceremony, their father will impart a great blessing for them and then he will release them into their adulthood. This ceremony is very meaningful and very important to every Jewish child. It is something that each child will look forward to with great expectation.

Over the last 25 or 30 years the Lord has been teaching me and preparing me with understanding and an anointing regarding the importance of releasing children into their adulthood and imparting a special blessing into them and all the divine power that this blessing carries from the Throne and heart of father God. When I was in Bible School, I read several hundred pages of writings by the revivalist called Charles Finney. I can still remember looking at a portrait of Finney with what seemed to be fire coming out of his eyes. It is recorded that Charles Finney went into a woman's factory one day and they were giggling at him and he looked at them and they came under such extreme conviction that they could no longer continue to do their work. So the factory owner asked Finney if he would have an evangelistic meeting at his factory, for it was useless to try to resume their normal work schedule. Many other stories abound regarding the extreme conviction that would accompany Finney at his meetings and the many souls that would be soundly converted and transformed. So, I decided this was the kind of ministry that I wanted to have and I can remember imagining about revival coming to places that I would visit, just like Finney. Absolutely, it was Finney for me and my future style of ministry.

Then, I would hear of people that would talk about "daddy" God and His love for us and it deeply bothered me. I now understand that the reason talking about "daddy" bothered me so much was because of my own unhealed issues in relationship to my father. I come from a very dysfunctional family. We were very religious and we always went to Church every week. My mom at times would take me as a little boy to Church at 530 in the morning! There was a lot of screaming and prejudice in my growing up years. I remember terms like "nigger" and "hillbilly" used on a regular basis. I did not want friction and it seemed at almost every holiday; like Easter and Christmas, someone would erupt in anger and get mad at someone else in the home. I used to hope and wish that maybe this year there would be no fighting, but it almost always seemed to end up with some fighting and screaming. Therefore, growing up in a large family with many brothers and sisters, there was much friction in the atmosphere and we all had unmet needs. Our parents also had these same needs and so they could not minister into our tremendous needs. The key that Satan used to stir up all the friction, I now know was a breakdown within the parental love. To put it simply, my parents did not choose to love each other. What is at the top will always filter down to all that is below.

At the time of age 19, I was radically saved and my vision was for a great revival. In fact, I was consumed with a passion for revival and before this time, I did not even understand the basic principles of Christianity. So, **Someone** put a desire inside of me to experience revival and I now realize that it was Father God. Here I was, a firebrand for a Finney type revival to take place in my lifetime and then I would hear some dear soul talk about Father Daddy God`s love for us. I thought, "what?" Daddy and revival do not go together. "Finney and revival, yes! Daddy and revival, Never!"

It seemed like I would try to stay away from those "daddy God" guys and read about Finney and other people similar to Finney. So, I continued to preach repentance and revival and I would see a lot of people repenting and confessing their sins regularly. I saw some fruit, but not a whole lot of fruit in my ministry. Then something started to change in my ministry. First, I started to go to inner healing Seminars and I started to get help for Greg Violi's soul. Once I started to get some very necessary balm for my soul, now I would start to pray for deep inner healing in others. This continued to get stronger and stronger within my life and ministry. One day, someone gave me a blessing from a father and I could hardly put my arms out to the brother that was blessing me, and therefore he wrapped his big arms around me. I did not feel much at all at this time, that this brother blessed me, and something definitely began to change within me.

Then one day, I started to give someone a father's blessing and they were deeply touched and I thought this is interesting. Although, so much was now changing inside of me, deep inside of my inner being, I would hear this inner voice whisper, "Finney and not Father". I said defiantly, "yes!", "Finney and not Father". As time went on, I started to see more and more lives being changed by giving them the blessing that their earthly father never gave them. Not only did I see more and more lives changed, but I myself started to feel more and more love and compassion for them and for all others. These transformed lives continued to increase and increase everywhere that I would go. Still, deep inside, my heart would say, "Finney and not Father". However, I still continued to see some amazing results! The Lord also continued to increase my understanding of the pain and the hurts that most people carry on the inside of them. Just like the writer of Ecclesiastes describes, *"So I returned, and considered all the oppressions that are done under the sun: and behold the tears of such as were oppressed, and they had no comforter; and on the side of their oppressors there was power; but they had no comforter."* (Eccl. 4:1). More and more I would actually see the hidden tears that many people had deep inside and I was learning that the majority of their tears were directly related to a father wound inside of them.

My heart started to break for more and more people and then I would hear the Father say that many of His children are lonely. They come to Church every week and they smile on the outside, but they are very lonely on the inside. They need to feel special and to feel loved. Then I discovered an amazing fact. There were at least 5 references in the New Testament of the proper way to greet one another.

1. "Salute one another with an holy **kiss**. The churches of Christ salute you." (Romans 16:16)
2. "All the brethren greet you. Greet ye one another with an holy **kiss**." (1 Cor 16:20).
3. "Greet one another with an holy **kiss**." (2 Cor. 13:12).
4. "Greet all the brethren with an holy **kiss**." (1 Thess 5:26).
5. "Greet ye one another with a **kiss** of charity. Peace be with you all that are in Christ Jesus. Amen." (1 Peter 5:14).

When the Lord says something once, its important and when He says it twice, its real important and when He says the same thing 5 times, we better do it! Why do we usually not greet one another with a holy kiss? Has a religious spirit told us not to kiss someone of the opposite sex. It says greet one another and it does not say men greet men and women greet women. There are millions of young girls that need a spiritual father to give them a pure, holy kiss of love. And there are millions of young men that need a spiritual mother to give them a pure, holy kiss of love. Father's intent has always been for spiritual fathers and spiritual mothers to fill His Body with His very own pure, holy love. One day, I was speaking at a well-known Bible School in Germany. My subject was spiritual fathers and mothers, while I was speaking on how Paul addressed and referred to his spiritual children as "beloved", "son", dearly beloved", and etc., I suddenly realized that no one had ever referred to me as son and I was 50 years old at that time.

The Father's cry seemed to get stronger and stronger inside of me for the family of God to really know their Father and His pure love. I must say that it took many, many years for me to totally decide that my ministry would not be a Finney style ministry, but instead a Father style ministry.

Now, in the year 2016, I have seen over 10,000 individuals deeply affected and many radically changed through a father blessing. I have seen multitudes of curses broken instantly, bodies healed, souls restored, joy restored, fears leave, depression healed, pain disappear, a new desire for life come where there was no hope or desire, marriages radically changed, and on and on. All these things happening as a result of receiving a father's blessing. It is and has been truly wonderful and amazing to behold the Father come to the deep places within His precious children and heal and restore and welcome them back into His heart of pure love! When once they felt so lonely, dishonored, and uncared for, suddenly within moments, they now feel honored, special, and cared for. I simply would not have ever believed such a thing was possible, but since I have personally seen it happen so many times, I must believe and teach the importance of men imparting a father's blessing to their children; in the natural and in the spirit. I am so thankful to my heavenly Father for all of His tremendous care, honor, and love He has towards his wounded children. Thank you Father God.

With this introduction as to how I came into the Father's Blessing understanding, I will now proceed to teach on some of the specifics concerning how the Father ministers to a person during the actual time of impartation and prayer.

The following guidelines are revelations and instructions that I have been given by God over the last 20 years basically to pray over people of all ages, nationalities, genders, and etc. These are just guidelines used while I am praying over each individual. I always do it one on one, the Holy Spirit also shows me other specific things about the person. This has increased as I have learned to just relax and listen to His voice and be a vessel for the Father to pour His own love through me.

I begin by knowing that each person coming for a father blessing is needing and wanting it and this is why they have come forward to receive it from me. They have an ache in their heart that only a blessing from a father can fulfill. Since Father God lives in each believer, any godly man can impart this extremely needed blessing in His name. (see Eph. 4:6).

The Prayer Blessing that is below will contain some personal words that I spoke to a Pastor after we had a Father Seminar, and I feel that it is important not to edit these words, but, instead to record them the way that I spoke them. Understanding that this was necessary is greatly appreciated. Thank you.

## THE PRAYER TO IMPART A FATHER'S BLESSING

Everyone yearns for their earthly father to bless them no matter how old they are, they still desire that their father will bless them.

Now if they come, and I start asking them questions, and they just shake their head up and down, and respond with, "yes yes yes yes," There are two main reasons why a person will just start nodding their head up and down. They are: 1. not yet ready to face their deep pain. 2. Fear of father or mother and they have adapted to their controlling and dominating parent by never thinking or saying no to them. They would be terrified to ever say no and therefore, they condition themselves to only say yes to whatever their parent (usually a father) desires of them. These children grow up living in fear based relationships, whereby fear is the controlling factor in all their relationships. They deeply fear not being accepted and not pleasing others. They are usually under sickness because fear triggers many illnesses in the human body. Also, they are not in touch with their true feelings and usually they have buried many of the painful and real feelings in their soul. Some parents will communicate that message to their children without ever speaking it. They have such a power that they will communicate to that child, "what I say goes and you will obey and what you say doesn't matter". And this is the main reason why some people that come for prayer cannot stop shaking their head while you are speaking to them. They are always shaking their head in the affirmative. Jesus said, "let your yes be yes **and** your no be no." So these dear people are afraid of ever voicing their **no** to others. It is ok to say no to people and sometimes it is absolutely essential that we do say no. These individuals will probably need another father's blessing when they are ready to deal with the pain in their souls.

When someone comes for a blessing and you look into her eyes and she starts to cry, she is about to be changed in about 5 minutes of prayer. Abba Father loves to come inside of these dear souls and bring his pure healing love to them. While you are looking into their eyes and they are crying, it is usually because Father is already removing pain from them. So at that point, just see yourself going out and God the Father coming into your vessel. Ephesians 4 says the Father is in you all, so the Spirit is in us and the Son is in us; but at this moment acknowledge the Father as dwelling in you. *"One God and Father of all, who is above all, and through all, and in you all."* (Ephesians 4:6)

Next, just reaffirm them that you are just going to do what their father should have done to them and smile with Abba's pure love in your eyes.

I always try to begin with, "will you forgive me?". They are carrying so much pain because their father has wounded them so much, and you can be sure that their earthly father never one time asked them for forgiveness. So at this moment things will start to happen because you are doing what he should have done.

"Will you please forgive me?" something is going to change right then. But then you're probably going to see some demons manifest. Usually, at this point there will be pain manifesting and maybe crying .You are going to see the pain and you are probably going to see a demon because many people believe a lie that they can't even think about the bad things that have happened to them as a child. The demons love it, because under that lie, there are demons that are hiding. Some of these spirits are unforgiveness, bitterness, hate, self-hatred, self-pity, and etc.

Now here is a wonderful thing about the father's blessing; it includes a tremendous impartation of God the Father, of His pure love, and it brings deliverance. It breaks curses and it heals the soul; and many times it will also bring healing to the body. That is what I have experienced with the father's blessing, it includes all of that. So you are now in the process of giving the father's blessing, and as long as they are secretly stuck in unforgiveness they are bound. So the first thing you want to do is to bring them into forgiveness; and that is canceling the ground Satan had; and in the spiritual realm it is all visible. So now what God the Father has been waiting 40 years maybe to do to this dear child of his, He can now do it.
(See Isaiah 30:18)

I have seen some women with murder and I have seen demons manifest in their eyes because they are so angry at their father; and then usually if I start to cry, this stronghold breaks immediately. But I can't make myself cry, it has to be Father God coming through me. Father God always suffers with anyone that is abused, especially when the abuser is a person that was designed by God to cover, love, and protect that dear one. Now, once this unforgiveness is broken; mercy and love and transformation has begun. One precious woman of God, many years ago said that all forgiveness involves the healing of memories. I think I would have to say a hearty amen to that statement. Yesterday, one of the ladies was going through a religious prayer with me and I had to stop her and help her enter into the reality of her heart and just be committed to the pure love of God, because the demons have trained us to just speak it out," I confess, I forgive, I forgive ..." She could not breathe because of the unforgiveness towards her mother. So instead of leading her into a religious formal kind of prayer which she was used to, I brought her into reality by telling her, "now see yourself in the heart of the Lamb, and be totally committed to that heart only." Since the heart is the key to deliverance and freedom, now she was released from the demonic entrapment. I brought her into reality, and everything that was blocking her breathing left. There has to be reality within a person's heart and it cannot only be a learned religious prayer.

Many times some of the people cannot go there at that moment, but in the next 2 minutes they will; so you do not have to wait for them to go there immediately because there is such a Presence over you and over them. Like one time in London I asked this girl if she could forgive me. The first thing she said was, "oh my father was good", and the Holy Spirit said "no", and he was horrible, and then I said, "will you forgive me?". She could not speak, and demons started to look through her eyes; then she started to hit me because she was so angry at her father. I knew at that moment that I desperately needed Jesus to manifest, and all my inner being was crying out to Jesus. Within one minute Jesus came, and she forgave him. So you have to be conscious of that tremendous Presence that loves that person extremely. Yes, He extremely loves that person. So if they can't speak it out, that is OK. Keep taking them into love, stay focused in God and say, "Will you forgive me?" and then say, "Will you release me for your father and for all the pain and disappointments that he has caused you?"

There are two things you want to try to get at. If they are real strict and have a mindless face and a real strict face, and they are going, "Yeah, yeah, I forgive you, I forgive you", they are not forgiving, they are just doing exactly what their father wants. "They are not going to get rid of the hell buried inside of their memories, and if demons are manifesting and they are crying and there is an atmosphere of heaven **and** hell, heaven will always win." I love that one truth, so you just stay in heaven, stay in God and you know that they are going to forgive, and they are going to release. There are two things to remember as a goal while you are praying with these individuals.

> Firstly – to forgive – *what the father did.*
> Secondly – to release – and this involves the *feeling he gave them* when he did it.

Releasing has to do with the feelings of dishonor that so many children carry from the way their fathers treated them.

eg. A man rapes a girl. That is what he did.
But then there is the way he made her feel when he raped her, and that is where most of the pain is located.

The devil will say, "You are a whore." They will tell that 6 year old girl, "You're a bad girl. You deserve that" and all kinds of other evil lies. But she needs to come to the truth, and with that tremendous presence of God over you, she will come to the truth, that she never deserved that, and that person and that father whoever he was, was evil, and he did not care about her feelings, and he totally dishonored her. Father God will communicate that through you, and that is when their whole world changes. So many individuals are carrying deep shame, guilt and worthlessness for no reason whatsoever.

Now it is all going to make sense for the person that is being blessed by you. The pain starts to come out and all kinds of stuff, like wounds and hurts as well. But you are communicating pure love with tremendous honor and blessing; and you want to always have that goal. Bring them to that place where they forgive and release. **Forgiveness** has to do with what the other person did to them and **release** has to do with how they made them feel when they did it. So you are standing there and you are saying, "Will you please forgive me for what I did, and release me for the way I made you feel?"

Many times I won't say, "I"; I'll just say, "the way your father made you feel". Sometimes people come up and they just love Greg Violi; and I know immediately they are not going to be able to relate to their father when they are looking at me. And God gives me wisdom, and I will say, "Will you please forgive your father?" But all the things that start happening in the spirit are way beyond comprehensive, and they are all related directly to their earthly father.

The first main thing is that you let them know, "I am standing in for your father to do what he should have done", because many of these poor innocent people actually believe that the way their father was; was OK and that is why my book on the Father is so important. That is why a seminar can help so much because God will show us from the Bible what an earthly father should be; and with the truth, you will become free. You will see that your father was probably a very bad person that was terribly selfish and irresponsible and a vessel for satan, instead of a vessel for Father God. You do not tell them that, but the Holy Spirit will reveal truth to them.

So here you are, giving a father's blessing, and you want to bring them to forgiveness and to release their father. And now once this is cleared away and they are usually falling and crying. You have got to have someone holding them up, because now it is time to impart the blessing! I usually will now say, "I want you to know that every word you speak is important, and every thought you have, because it comes from you and you are important."

Most of their fathers have never communicated that to any of them, "and you are not a mistake, you are not an accident and you are not a burden." At that point I break a lie that almost everyone has carried; and it is from the liar, and this lie says, "You do not deserve to be living, and you have to prove it." You will be amazed at how many people have that lie. How does it manifest when we carry that lie? There will be tension in the lower spine and a lot of stress and struggle in your nervous system and in the body. That person is constantly fighting that lie. In their spirit they are saying, "I deserve to be alive," but the lie says, "You don't, you have to prove it." The spirit says, "I deserve to be alive," the lie says, "You don't", and it makes life real difficult. But, "In the name of Jesus and in the power of his blood, I command the stress to go out of that body. Many times I can feel that stress leaving the spine.

I myself had two lies that I carried for many years:
1. I don't deserve to be alive
2. I don't deserve to speak.

So if the parent ever says, "Be quiet", "Shut up", "Children should be seen and not heard". All of these phrases bind that precious child and prevents him from expressing what is on their heart and the creative ability of Almighty God is blocked. About 6 weeks ago we had a lady in this room, with a few others. I was praying with the one and then the other. And then this one was totally quiet, and she is a nice woman, she loves God, she loves Jesus; and now it is time for them to go and the Lord says, "Say something to her, get her to talk." She is very nice, she is from Poland, a very Catholic country, and she started to talk, and I cannot remember what she said, but she had major pain and extreme fear. And I guess if I remember correctly, she had a spirit from Catholicism. She could not receive the baptism of the Holy Spirit; she could not open her mouth, she was dominated. So I prayed, broke it over her and I found out about a month later that since that day she is totally changed. She has witnessed to many people and she is alive to Jesus. It is amazing. So when it comes to Catholicism you need to break the ungodly soul tie with the Vatican. It is an ungodly tie. It could easily control a person and prevent her from feeling freedom to just speak and release the love of the Father into the world.

## BACK TO THE FATHER'S BLESSING

You communicate in this blessing that they are important, and you break that lie, and you command the stress to go. Now if there has been trauma, emotional, physical, or sexual; there is a link with the headquarters of Satan, the second heavens, so you ask the Lord

Jesus to break the link with the second heavens and their trauma. That link is very similar to ungodly soul ties and the devil will come through that demonic link and he will keep triggering them at their points of trauma. But once the link is broken, you now command the spirit of trauma and stress to go out of their body, because the spirit of stress has been triggering them in many areas like in the adrenal glands; and then you have the pituitary gland that is inside of your brain, and these little tiny glands are so very important for all the different tasks that they fulfill in your body.

There is no specific order. I am just telling you the way God has been leading me over the years. The more you give the father's and mother's blessing, (I've given it about 15,000 times), the more you give it, the more you learn and the easier it becomes. The first 20 times, it could be hard, but still the Father will communicate His love, but I am giving you a lot. So in that blessing there is authority now, which is straight from Father, a divine authority that comes from heaven and it gets really fun. You break curses of rejection. When I do it I know it is broken. And many times they say, "We have done all that". Well, even though they might say that I have done all of that, just do it again with them. Many of these believers have done all of these blessings and prayers, but still there is very little fruit. The great news is that today, we are living at a time when the Father himself is coming and releasing his blessing and replacing the curses that so many earthly fathers put onto their precious children. A few weeks ago, while I was releasing the father's blessing, I heard Father God say, "arrested development". I thought I have had no dealings with this spirit in many years and the last time, "I tried" to deal with it, it did not seem to have much fruit. But, suddenly the heavenly King and Father comes and says arrested development. It is as if God steps down into the room and says, "excuse me son, I now want to deal with a spirit that has caused a lot of trouble for my precious children." In the next few days, about 15 people were set free from this spirit and there were dramatic results in their lives. A complete freedom in areas such as insecurity, fear, pain, and many other things. Arrested development will come into your life and he will arrest your development and therefore, you may be 45 or 65 years old; but on the inside, your abilities (body, soul, mind) are completely stifled and locked up. This could come because of a controlling father or mother that never allows their child to make decisions and to have choices, but instead, they always tell their child what to do.

There is another curse that some people come under and it is called, the vagabond curse. *"Whoso rewardeth evil for good, evil shall not depart from his house."* (Prov. 17:13).

*"Behold, thou hast driven me out this day from the face of the earth; and from thy face shall I be hid; and I shall be a fugitive and a **vagabond** in the earth; and it shall come to pass, that every one that findeth me shall slay me."* (Gen 4:14)

*"Let his children be continually **vagabonds**, and beg: let them seek their bread also out of their desolate places."* (Psalm 119:10).

When someone does evil to you in return for your good, and that is what always happens with an abusing or controlling father and his child, this vagabond curse will come on you. It is a very serious thing and then you will feel like a vagabond. You feel like you never fit in. You may be the pastor of a Church, but in your heart you do not feel like you fit in. I was talking to a well-known singer in South Africa about the vagabond curse and the Lord was lifting it off of her while I was talking and she cried and cried. She was delivered just talking about it. The vagabond curse will always make someone feel that they just do not fit in, so they always have a lonely look on their face. It is believed that the Gypsy bloodline is directly related to Judas that betrayed Jesus. I am not certain if this true, but this is what I have heard and read.

So you are releasing all this blessing and breaking these curses. You let them know how important they are. At this point I say, "I release you from that inner feeling of being a little boy or a little girl, and I call you into your adulthood. Call them into their adulthood because that is the father's job to affirm their gender and to release them into adulthood. Call them into their true self. Please understand how powerful the word in your mouth is, and you have that authority and so does every earthly father. You call them into their true self; you call them into life and to fulfill their destiny. The more the faith of God comes in with this blessing, the more you have the attitude of Isaac. When he blessed Jacob instead of Esau, he then said he shall be blessed. *"And Isaac trembled very exceedingly, and said, Who? where is he that hath taken venison, and brought it me, and I have eaten of all before thou camest, and have blessed him? yea, and he shall be blessed."* (Genesis 27:33) And this is what is in me every time I give a blessing. I know they are going to be blessed and they will never be the same. And this is amazing because this is a man that did not even want to think about a father's blessing, and now he sees phenomenal results. This is the way God does it, and this is a man who never really had any relationship with his own father, and never knew a spiritual father and came from a dysfunctional family. This is what grace is all about and it glorifies the Father.

So you are calling them into life. You are just about done now. Then usually I will give them their honor back. I just say, "I give your honor back, the honor that has been taken away from you,

I give it back. And then maybe just one more thing and I think this is the most important. This I think has the greatest effect. The pure love of Abba Father is so real and powerful, but it needs to be felt and not just talked about. These dear children desperately need to feel the touch of a father's arms and maybe his lips on their shoulders and face. I will literally see the Father God coming through my arms, through my lips, through my heart and just consuming them. And I will hug them and I will kiss them with all the strength that I have. It is not religious, it is extremely real and there can be no fear. I kiss a lot of beautiful women and you have to be in agreement with your spouse before you do this. If a man does this, he must have the okay from his wife. Those "wonderful" religious spirits will let you know how you should never do that. Can I tell you something? These people with these religious spirits probably have a lot of uncleanness, pride, jealousy, and hate; and because of their unclean hearts, they are not willing to be a vessel for Father God to love others through them. And now they are trying to tell us not to get too close to the opposite sex and to never kiss anyone of the opposite sex because of the "standard of holiness".

It is an abomination and there is no reality, and the Holy Spirit with many Scriptures has taught me the opposite. He has taught me how important it is to hug and to kiss, especially in this day and in this hour because there is so much abuse. And this is probably the time where we need the greatest number of spiritual fathers ever in the history of humanity. And I think maybe there is a mandate from heaven now to start kissing and hugging. Now He told us 2,000 years ago. But we are holy! Are we holy or are we rebellious, proud, wicked, insensitive, and uncaring. I think that many leaders have covered themselves with human goodness and have called it holiness and the heart of God is saddened.

So you see that is it, and you see why you have to be out, it is so easy if you are out. Does the Father want to bless? Does the Father want to break every curse? Does the Father want to heal the soul? Does the Father want to embrace? Does the Father want to honor? Does the Father want to kiss? Well if the prodigal son was a true story, He does!

AMEN!

## A CLOSING PRAYER OF IMPARTATION TO RELEASE A FATHER`S BLESSING TO OTHERS

*"Father God, I ask you in the name of your precious Son Jesus, to release now into all willing hearts your purest love and compassion and anoint each person reading this now with the power of your Spirit to impart a father`s blessing (a man) and a mother`s blessing (a woman). I remove all fear and I release you right now to start to release the heart of the heavenly Father into the world, first with those individuals that are closest to you. You are now empowered by Father God and anointed with His Spirit to reveal His deep desire to love, honor and bless his children. "*

Your servant,
Greg Violi

# Other life changing Books available from Pastor Greg Violi:

### *Depression and Introspection: Healing for the diseased mind:*
This book explains root causes for depression and how the disease of introspection affects millions. Greg shares from the Word of God how depression blocks a person from living in the presence of God and how a you can walk in freedom it.

### *The Lamb's Heart*
This book is a thorough revelation of the spiritual heart of man and the heart of God. It contains many truths concerning brokenness in the father's heart and how to allow the father to heal your own brokenness. There is a tremendous revelation about how and why God always looks at the heart of man.

### *The King's Holy Beauty*
This book is a revelation of the secret mystery hidden in the heart of Father God. This revelation from the Holy Spirit is to unveil the beauty of God`s holiness. Since this book has been published there have been many testimonies of the changed lives of the people who have read it.

### *Whose Image and Which mind*
This book discusses the differences between heavenly and earthly wisdom, the heavenly image and the earthly demonic image. Through this book you can discover the splendor of living life through the heart of the Lamb of God! Living a life after God´s heavenly design and being fed from the river of divine wisdom!

### *Called to be kings and Priests*
In this book the purpose of a godly father and husband are revealed through the scriptures. It is also reveals how to live out God's divine design and purposes of a man practically. Through revelation from God´s Word you will also learn how to heal wounds created by men not fulfilling God's calling on men.

### A Heavenly Victorious life

The Spirit of the ascended Christ desires to come inside of a believer and reveal himself. When we allow him to reveal himself through us; it produces a heavenly life, a life that is always abounding in victory. Greg describes the real life of the ascended, exalted Lord and how we can abide in the fullness that he offers.

### The Key to Staying in Love

God desires mercy more than any sacrifice that man can offer. In any relationship, the most desirable attributes are kindness, mercy, and love. When a person allows appearance or possessions to take first priority in a relationship, judgements and hardness replace a heart attitude of kindness and love. The love of God cannot abide where there is hardness of heart. In this small booklet, you can learn how judgements operate and how to guard yourself from such destructive attitudes.

### Finding Father

Father God desires that His children experience His loving embrace on a daily basis. He intended every earthly father to bless his children and release a deep sense of purpose and identity into them King David said the gentleness of God was the secret to him being great. (Psalm 18:35). When someone tastes the goodness and gentleness of God, pains are healed, hope is restored and life takes on new meaning.

---

You can find other messages and seminars from Pastor Greg Violi on Youtube under Greg Violi Ministries.

For more information about Greg Violi Ministries and Greg's Itinerary visit his website at:

www.greg-violi.com

Made in the USA
Lexington, KY
13 February 2017